Faces of Eve

ALSO BY R. W. STEDINGH

Poetry

Faces of Eve
From a Bell Tower
The Stanley Park Suite

Translation

Arved Viirlaid: Selected Poems
(with T. E. Moks)

R. W. STEDINGH

Faces of Eve

REVISED EDITION

LYRE Press
Vancouver
1999

LYRE Press
P. O. Box 88333
523 Main Street
Vancouver, B. C. V6A 4A6

Canadian Cataloguing in Publication Data

Stedingh, R. W., 1944-
      Faces of Eve

Rev. ed.
Previously published as: Ashes: poems/by R. W. Stedingh, A, McMillan. Halifax, N. S. : Phoenix Pub., 1969
Poems.
ISBN 0-9685172-0-X

      I. Title

PS8587.T424A8 1999   C811'.54   C99-900432-8

for Thea de Vos

ACKNOWLEDGEMENTS

Some of these poems originally appeared in a provisional document entitled *Faces of Eve*, which in turn appeared in *Ashes* (Phoenix Publications: Halifax) 1969, a joint-edition of poems by Arvo McMillan and myself. Within a year, this edition of *Ashes*, and thus *Faces of Eve*, was out of print. It is for that reason that after thirty years this second, revised and greatly expanded edition is published. Most of the poems have been extensively rewritten, and a considerable number of new poems have been added to the collection.

Some of the new poems in this revised edition were originally published in literary magazines as follows: "Sun" in *Abraxas* (USA); "For a Moment," "Sirens," "Virgin" and "Penelope" in *Northern Light*; "Question" in *PRISM international*; "Flamenco" and "An Old Love Story" in *Quarry*; "Signs" in *Scopcraeft* (USA); "Noon Window" in *The Canadian Forum*; "Akimbo" in *The Far Point*; "A Voice in Winter" in *The Malahat Review*; and "Pigalle" in *The Tamarack Review*. "Birds of Memory" and "Nocturne" originally appeared in an anthology edited by Robert Sward, *Cloud Nine: Vancouver Island Poems*, (Victoria: The Soft Press), 1973.

"A Voice in Winter" won the MacMillan Prize for Poetry at the University of British Columbia in 1971.

CONTENTS

I.

II.

III.

I.

*All things are an exchange for fire and fire for all things,
as goods are for gold and gold for goods.*

Herakleitos, Fragment 90

FOR A MOMENT

When night is about to vanish,
Just before dawn,
And any "Who goes there?"
Goes unanswered,

The half-light opens,
Fog lifts like smoke
Over the river,

And on the bridge
I listen
To the endless quiet
Of a woman:

Our distances blend,

And as if carried away
We remain.

SUN

At daybreak, the stars
Go out in the sky,
And the great display of the comets
Ceases over the equivocal horizon
Upon which one may lose his way in the light.

Midday holds its breath,
And when the ground shakes with palsy
At an unknown distance,
I know over the city
Mirages are still practicing.

Tonight they will fly
As high as their shadows throw them;
Tonight they will land
Just beyond melancholy.

SIREN

A dead child crying saltless tears;
A weeping statue.

What else, then, could she be
But in her absence so insisting
She requires no one,
A headless rider,

And rattles her trick-chains
In the dark,
Each link for a new limb
She is trying to grow.

Still wondering what I live on,
How would she know?

With her surmises
Death would be my only justice,
But in her world
Who would want to be a man

Or a woman
For that matter?

VIRGIN

"The first time," she said,
"How could I in a light so blinding be
Expected to remember anything?
Drowning in a high sea, I found myself
Floating eyeless in the night sky
With stars on the corneas of my eyes.
Like crystals, they were converging
Through a window without touching,
Or luminous sea creatures
Rising from the depths to see again.
And after, rain hissing in swells
As the deep itself rose to greet me
In the silence between our two houses.

"But it is nothing we have come to,
My Love, and to nothing we return,
Except for the tingling, my body's
Memory of it still in the room,
And the sense of being inside-out
And outside-in, of being both, of neither
Till your voice with its care became
A life-buoy I no longer need, but am.

"How I have come to hate it: the broken mirror
Of me beyond myself—
What you can never be—
Addicted as you are to the rightness of earth
And solid ground, to my facing the full mask
Of your desire, and to my endless dying there
As here what happens happens without me.

"Though I be the door, though you believe
And disbelieve, I insist impossibilities."

PENELOPE

She hides in twilight,
Shedding, picking and beating in,
And the great wind stops and breathes,
Stops and breathes merely,
In the shadow of a man.

From time to time
She watches the horizon
Changing with the sea
As if someone were lost there
Like the uncertain son
In the absence of absence.

Yet she weaves wise garments,
Binds what she can, keeping cold,
And like a good wife
Frequently whimpers over the tapestry
Saying, "This, only this
Is for you,"

The warp lines up like dead men,
The weft curves in like dead men,
And she faces the shuttle
Of a threadless day
Weaving and unweaving it

Until the sailor
Emerges from the loom.

MADAME BEATRICE

Not someone out of Dante who was never found
Beyond her false mystery and distance
In which she thrived, always adding
Another brick to the wall,
Warding off the beloved, keeping him pining
And forever at bay. No. This Beatrice
Is all intimacy and truth, although
She is not a madame either, turned vicious,
Of the war. Here in the cool morning,
I climb two flights of stairs to her run-down room
On a back street of Ile Saint-Louis, where she struggles
With the dark in the room and survives,
Naked from the waist up and full-breasted,
Nursing her infant like a haggard Madonna
Sobbing and asking me for money I don't have.

We talk, she in broken English,
I in broken French, but all she remembers,
As if just waking up, is her obscure lover
Whose lies of his love were his only truth,
Though he seemed to have a mission,
Whose eyes flashed like sheet-lightning,
Like an angel of the Lord, when he saw her.
We try to piece the past together with words
In languages we are not sure of
Only to find the sordid present:
Wall paper peeling in coils from the wall
Down to the holes in the broken floor,
The toilet yawning its broken bowl
As the tungsten wire in the bare light bulb
Pings and goes out.

And in the dark shade of the room
We hear the child, without its mystery, crying,
The child she decides she will give up
To the world.

FLAMENCO

The guitarist holds *La Duana*
By the throat,
And rubs his elbows into wood
As nylon wires
Like threads of spittle
Lick his fingers
Where the knuckles bleed.

Around him, in candlelight,
The singer comes and goes:
A voice of sandpaper walking
Between ends of a board.

Yet the music curls
And crackles
Like a red leaf under
The dancers' dresses.
They suck their tongues
Like cats in heat,
Arch their arms
And freeze the song
In the acid clap
Of castanets.

THE MIRACULOUS MANDARIN

The ruffians wait unseen in the shadows behind the lovely girl standing bare-breasted at the window. As the mandarin stops below her, she is repulsed by his mysterious, yellow figure.

Yet she dances wildly in the open window to distract him, and the mandarin's reserve is transformed into feverish excitement.

He mounts the stairs; she opens the door; he tries to embrace her. But her companions who have been lying in wait rush out, rob him and decide to kill him. Three times they stab with their daggers, but he does not bleed, and his longing for the girl is stronger than death.

Finally, she ceases to resist and responds to his embrace.

Only in her arms, fulfilled, do the wounds begin to bleed till at last he dies.

ARCHAIC TORSO OF THE VENUS DI MILO

The Louvre

Kicked up by the plough, the guide says,
This one born of surf flaming, white heat becoming
Not the spiralled nacre but the pearl,
Her hips still full and tasting
Of the unknown chisel.

And yet, no wound betrays the loss
Of her shell (save the chipped nipple
And the floating rib) like these absent arms,
If ever they were hers
(The right supposed holding up
A slipping drape, the left,
The golden apple of the isles),
Or,
Whether without them she was always
Meant to be
And, therefore, ever larger than imagined,
For with these invisible limbs she always did embrace
In wavering default like a magnet
The iron filings of the stoutest hearts
Till upright again and on a pedestal
She stands
Not as something born again,
Transformed or mended, but as always
Meant to be in this place she occupies,
In tender pugilism still,
Her vanquished about her
Like furniture, suddenly revealed
And fated to lose all ambivalence
(Of which she is queen).

Though once she was the cause of war,
All peace obeys as she feigns all
Direction without moving,
Her melting gaze, now blind,
Seeing inward sees all in polychrome,
She whose pose remains as ever
A boulder of white marble
Standing in the cliff-face,
Threatening fall, but knowing
She will always find someone to save her.

Even now, the wild shimmer of light
On her shoulders, formed domestic,
Is otherwise. But you will never know:
The source of her sweetness, begging kind,
Hones the silence and awe under her tongue
Which is true, is gold,
Is like no other.

PIGALLE

I.

Hairdresser of the world,
I spread my fingers, unconcerned,
I a woman's soapy hair
I crack white eggs in a Pyrex bowl,
Mixing with warm shampoo
An ancient father's recipe
For foaming heads obscure.

For all I know, I
May be feeding a Medusa
The rich albumen of my days,
For this head feels like all the rest
Sucking my hands and fingernails white.

Slosh   slosh
Slurp   slurp,
Tangle of my hands in her hair,
Tangle of her hair in my hands:

Children are bells that cannot chime
The unborn hopes of time.

II.

This glass bowl lies on a human table,
Heat-resistant, clear, unbreakable.
Surely, it is not a common cup,
Surely not a grail,
And, surely, these are not the hands of Christ,
Nor this longing that of Lancelot—

Although this place feels like Camelot,
Its main hall looming like a cave—
For I must kneel in soggy loam
Beside an old king's grave.

It is difficult to listen to,
Between the headstone and the sheet,
The heartless disappearance, the silence
Of his ghost that cannot smile or weep.

"The swallow has flown from the castle
Into a holy wood;
It lives with leaves and hides its head
Inside a darksome hood."
So goes the legend, cryptic and foreboding,

And this glass bowl is nothing without eggs,
A crystal ball that warns me not of myself
But of my love—to keep a human pace
And walk as if on the human face.

The children sing in overtones
A song that casts no stones.

III.

A great, grey eagle brought me here
Whose food my body has been,
And like Sinbad the Sailor
Or Sinbad the Failer,
I spend great morsels of my thighs
On passing birds,
Hanging my dreams on wire coat hangers
In the clouded closets that I pass,

For I am here
Among frothing shadows
And hair dryers in a line,
Combing a sunburst of cobras
In a dark woman's hair.

The children are singing songs in time
To the organ in my mind.

IV. *The Moulin Rouge*

The cracks in the cobblestones
Open their mouths at sundown.

Walking walkways with masked hopes,
Hoping that the price is not too high,
Timid with hands in fathomless pockets,
Trying in my mind what I might say
To materialized dreams in bright underclothes,

I ask what the world demands:
Phantasmagoric wish from me
That is not in the pomegranate seed.

In the damp night
Neon hisses in glass veins.
Its red tongue of light licks
The tears on a young girl's face,
And as her steel heel
Caught between paving stones
Sinks deeper,
The four arms of the sign
Roll over her like a cross.

If I have said it before
Over dead bodies at funerals,
I am saying it again:

She died with much relief
As she returned without blame
To that soft, melancholy whisper
Whence she came.

But there is too much black ink in the air
To see the white hairs in the woman's head I pass.
She lingers in a doorway with her fur
And the white domes of the Sacre Coeur.

She is old,
She is young.
She licks my eyeballs
With her tongue.

She wriggles,
And her body laughs
With hand-cupped breasts
That do a rubber dance,

And her teeth
Have found me
Deep
Inside.

O let me touch you,
Wife to me,
To no one
And to all!

In my veins I feel a rope go slack.
A boat pulled up a river
Capsizes in my head, and the question
I do not ask myself is answered
By the lines that draw old faces.

The choired voices of children sing
The songs that do not rhyme.

V. *A Side Street*

I am walking shoeless in the muddy sea
And feel it all between my toes
What lies there in the gutter
Between the Hotel Lux
And the *Ecole de jeunes filles*:
The rat eyes scamper and squeak
Through soggy tissues and candy-bar wrappers
To copulate in the stream of toilets.

Beggars are in the street
Selling their reputations like hot popcorn
To the visiting sons of the American revolution
Who buy a promise with a promise.

"*Le voila!*"
"*Oui!*"
"*Ha-ha-ha!*" comes the chant of the bourgeoisie,
Voyeurs fingering their Beaujolais
In a sidewalk cafe, watching crew-cut Quasimodos climb
A stairway in a ramshackle whore house:
Again, cheers rise up from the cobblestones
As the enlightened fall as the fallen fall

Like eggs
On the sidewalk which will leave no trace
Of even the wet footprints of the rats.

When the children sing,
The song becomes a whine.

VI.

And I watch too. The padded chests
Come forth with rasping beaks,
Charging on the already eaten,
Throwing plastic flowers on their graves,
Relaxing the tired tentacles of hope:

And I must clog my pipe stem with spittle
And drink it dragging dreams from a bowl
As large as the inside of my head,
Afraid I might be tapped on the shoulder,
Afraid I might be getting older.

The children sing an epithalamion,
But none are wedded, and none go on.

VII.

The world is not the earth which speaks
Louder to the heart, but what the world is
Is surreal with broken mirrors:

The elephant scares the mouse,
The fox flees Pertelote, and Chanticleer
Struts a fanned display in a world of crumbs;
The cucumbers run through the elephant patch,

28

Salad for the elephant trunks. All's unnatural;
All's grey; all's reversed. And for us
It is all one
Thieving victim frantic on a funny farm.

In the erehwon of the moment
An old God's grey beard drivels
Left-over, mongoloid slime.
His throne is a kingdom of urine;
His eyes are blinded with brine.
Ergo: Wisdom makes gods blind
When the wisdom is without love?
Or is it blindness makes one wise?
Or is it wise for wise men to grow fierce,
To grovel for the raiment of His corpse?
And what will they find but chards of pottery
We are bound to take for the God's crushed bones?
Ergo: No unhoping or unfriending man
Can out-bark them and their dry mouths
Nor give anchor to the grappling abstraction.

When the children sing, our ears
Are full of wax. We cannot hear.

VIII. *La Slavia Restaurant*

One must eat. There is yet time to eat
Whatever can be eaten with a knife.

Yet must we put napkins on our laps,
Expecting things to fall
From forks tenaciously portioned with our peas?

What danger lurks near the restaurant table

That the hand must shake, the food tumble,
The wine spill out over the checkered tablecloth?

Does the waiter serve it with my meal?
Or is it there with the breadcrumbs on the cloth
That I must chew my carrots with a cringe?

What breeding have our infants got
That sucks the marrow from their bones
And fills them with timorous steel?

I am eating; I am pressed,
Pressed with impossible things to do.
There is only time to nibble and to suck
The tired flesh and tendons
Of a boiled chicken's wing.

Soon, perhaps, the children
Will not sing.

IX. *The Prostitute*

I have lain this way before
In the strange bed of an old hotel,
Sandwiched in the cold sheets with my teeth
Chattering like dry seeds in a gourd.

I hear the bathroom water push
Through rattling pipes in a rotting floor
And grunt like a constipated ghoul
As the bidet fills behind the door.

It is a prelude to the metal snaps,
The release of straps

That strangle strange, elastic skin.

Yet I must wait
Waiting for the water to clear
And listen to the fall of clothes:
Her ankles crack, her bone joints creak,
She pulls her tired thighs of hose.

And what I see I know there is no cure for.
Wrapped in red silk, it seems to throb,
Froth and bubble, almost speak,
Like lava under the crust of a cool volcano.
And her skin is cracked like mud on cow udders
As she prods her way on padded feet and pretense
Into bed and gropes the bed sheets with a sigh:

>"*Quel grandeur, mon fil!* she says
>And repeats: "*Quel grandeur...*
>*Quel grandeur...*
>*Quel....*"

But her words are like her hands,
Sanitary as a probing physician
Expecting a cough.

I rest myself
Surrounded in her arms
And see the bones in shoulders
Hug the rhythm, hug the hope
And feel the progress
Of the spreading room.

Now when I hear the children sing,
Their voices ring like the wings
Of an immortal, human thing.

X. *Morning Song*

At dawn I am in a room that is not mine,
My feet up on the empty, sagging bed.
Burglars have entered in the night.

The wicker chair with the sunken seat,
The radio bought on time that did not play,

The piggy bank with the broken slot
Where I had spent amourous centimes:

All that is not mine is stolen.

XI.

Now I have nothing and no hope,
Nothing but coarse language
To put a hoarse world off,
And I must wait like dandruff
On the balding age of my head.

But with lilies in my lungs
And roses on my tongue,
I wash, tint, set or perm,
My fingers always in her hair like snakes,
And though I feel the sloth of stone
Gather in the blood around my heart, it is hers,
Broken early, went bad enough to stop men
In their tracks.

XII. *Envoi*

In blank cafes and rented rooms I roam
Listening to chalk-handed, drunken gnomes
Battle Medusa with biblical combs
As I curse the God or gods and goddesses
Who cursed her to this curse
Where I continue countering her power
With a head-message, the odd flower
And deep-song, a desperate verse.

FIRST LOVE

for Eileen Dickinson

I.

Tonight there is a storm.
Lightning flashes on the walls,
And thunder crashes
On the roof beams overhead.
The sound going through me
Keeps me awake.

I reach for your hand in the dark
And find it.

II.

My eye rests
Above your hip where the smooth
Rise slopes inward,
And my tongue follows
The warm sides
Of each of your folds.

In the young year
Again I am thankful
For your ample breasts,
And I hold your toes and ankles,
Kiss the backs of your knees,
Draw them apart.

Through the hours of the night
I carry in my mouth

The taste of you,
You who rise to me
Like waves of thunder
Calling me,

And I wonder why all this time
You have hidden from me,
Why have I ever hidden from you.

III.

In the sound of your heavy breathing
I feel the tips of your fingers,
Your thighs and the tight, moist hair:

We come to the same words
In the same voice
Knowing it is ours:

The earth is a lyre
That resonates in you,
In me, in us together:
Our bodies move
Like vibrating strings.

IV.

I know the hard stones of your bones,
The vertebrae like sharp boulders
In the valley of your back,
The silky mound of your belly,
The smooth birch bark of your throat,
The twisting river of your muscles
And the thunder in your veins,

Know the whole landscape of your eyes
Flashing with your mind's inner light.

Once there were many days and nights,
And then there was only yours and mine.

V.

When we open our eyes
To each other,
It is morning.

No one will ever see you
As you appeared
When I woke.

In the early light I lie watching
Your face asleep
On the same pillow:

I want to be the dream
You feel
And the light you wake to.

AN OLD LOVE STORY

As the gates flew open
The lovers entered
The house they entered,
And an old lady rocked
Herself off the porch.

Yet they were happy,
Holding hands,
Gripped by a dialogue
They could not grasp or hold.

When the balustrade
Guided their steps
To an empty room,
A match was struck
Under a table toward evening,
And the clipped wings of sparrows
Beat on the hips of the roof.

But still they were happy
In the burning room,
Embracing an old love story,
Dying each one alone.

CHATEAU DE BOUDRY

An elegant dinner-dance
In a medieval castle, the pig served
With a fanfare of trumpets,
An apple in its mouth.

And after the *repas*,
Sweet Molly from Texas,
A student of mine,
Asks me to dance.

And I hug her
For all she is worth,
And she hugs me
For all I am worth.

And my warm body
And her warm body
Move to the same beat
As the band plays on

Till the music stops.

TEACHING

Every day, another girl
Puts an apple on my desk
Just to see me eat it
Core and all.

MOLY

A plant, perhaps, or the powder
Of a white, wilted flower,
Its black root burrowing in the earth.
But more likely, the chipped bones of trees
Crushed into a mash, flattened and left
To bake in the sun,
To harden in the cold Alpine air.

It is found in speech which flies
Like a crow among owls, or
In rare, medium-rare and well-done books,
Darting like an owl among crows.

It is, in fact, the powdered scab
Coagulating like thought around a heart
That has scorched its valves,
Tied itself into half-hitches and square knots
And exploded, a heart cauterized
By the dry heat of the desert.

It is the pulverized scalpel of the mind
Dissecting a corpse that sleep-walks
In the light of night, the dark of day,
And never awakens.

These days, one must pour it
Into every libation
To intuit whether the ore she came from
And the coin she's become
Are legal tender.

II.

And I will put enmity between thee and the woman, and between thy seed and her seed; it shall bruise thy head, and thou shalt bruise his heel.

Genesis 3:15

FOUR SONGS FOR LINDA

I.

I squeezed a pimple
And walked with men,
Spotted with scabs
And chained like a criminal.
Hair vests, shoes of sod
And the wool of sacrificed lambs,
Kept warm their hearts of weeds,
And with mandrake roots
In their cracking mouths,
They lashed me,
Bathed me in the spit of crowds.

Your frail hand
Threw me a flower.

II. *Akimbo*

Akimbo, akimbo, akimbo.
Always your arms are akimbo.
Why not over your head or
Somebody's head or behind
Your head waiting or resting
Under your breasts or like
Simon says...all over?

It's an easy pose, though,
Waiting to be turned over like an hourglass
Or a clothes-tree to be fitted.

III. *When*

When you take my hand away,
The wind clicks with ice on the window,
The candle burns out on the table,
The clock falls off the wall
And crashes to the floor.

And at night, alone in the glacial bed,
I awaken to my shivering self.
It is the time when the teeth of the dead fall out,
And I remember that I am dying,
That I am the reason,
And my words are the garment
I wear in a nightmare
Like the tucked pant-leg
Of a one-legged boy.

IV. *A New Fable*

Like Eve in the fable
Only you believe,

You run
In your mini skirt
Across the clearing:

Glimpses of your
Underwear.

And
Nothing
More.

So I chase you
Until there is no one
Left to catch,

Until I have your heart
By heart.

FOG

What coastline, my Love,
Will not cloud over
If looked at long enough?

The needle
Still swings to a violent north
And goes round and round in circles:

We have arrived at the pole:
We cannot be saved here.

THE COMMON COLD

I move into you
As through a winter landscape,
My feet sinking in the snowdrift
Of your stares, waiting to be held
By more than your cold.

I traverse the drifts of your indifference
To my body and my love
Till I am waist-deep in snow:
The slow creek of your sex
Is frozen, and my hand
Freezes exactly there.

I wander in the forest of your mind
And become ensnared like a rabbit
In the understorey vegetation
By the invisible wire around your heart:
The more I struggle, the tighter
The noose around my neck,

For while my love is naked as a spring flower
Doing push-ups in the snow,
You insist on my being something else—
A meek sacrifice, a charging bull, or both—
Whispering in my ear,
"That's how the cold begins."

NUDE

The form, shape and symmetry
Of your impeccable body
Hide the gist of your love
Which comes out again and again
Like a bouquet of glass flowers
That shatters those who smell it.

My hand shakes in the darkness
Of the frame of mind in which you hide.

And I wonder where is the nude
Descending the staircase
Whose angular love and beauty fracture
The cool light in the eye of the beholder.

And you hear me from far away,
A voice that does not touch you.

AN HONESTY

When you get undressed,
You are an apple peeling
In front of the mirror
Leaving only your white flesh
In an outer skin
Of red lace underwear:

When you put your hand
In your panties and your finger
To your sex, pressing the stem
Till you throb,
The likeness in the glass
Is yourself
Trying not to be moved.

PETITE HISTOIRE

I am telling you how beautiful you are.
The curves of your legs draw me in
To your biblical dark—for that is what
You have made it, and your soft belly
Slides against mine.
I cup your pear-shaped breasts,
Kiss your full lips, spread
My fingers in your long black hair:
I'd do anything to keep you warm.

When you ask me what I'm doing,
As if there were something wrong,
I tell you, "Love, I'm making love
Rather than fucking you like an animal."

But you prefer seeing me as nothing
But a man.

SIGNS

I.

Tears in your eyes
Dry on the pillow

And leave no trace
Of the river inside

But black flowers
On your pillow case

Where the flake
Of your lashes

Is a delta of ashes,
And darkness drifting

Over a candle
Rubs out the light

Before midnight.
But there are other signs.

The bed makes a noise
With your moving away.

Your distance is measured
By a moaning spring.

II.

When the night gets hungry,
Wallpaper peels into blindness,
And a flickering flame
Is buried in wax
As the candle lies down.

And somewhere, under the ceiling,
My hands groping find
You begin where I end.

III.

It is late. The old man
In the room upstairs
Has dropped
His shoes on the ceiling.
Two echoes fall into the room
And chase each other
Around the walls
And over the mirror
As if no one were here,

Perhaps he will hear me snoring;
Perhaps he will hear you snoring.
Perhaps he will dream about
Two people in a bed,
Snoring.

A VOICE IN WINTER

I.

Snow: angel teeth falling
On the meadow's lap
In the time of blizzards;

Soul the raindrops
Freeze into
When the dead live,
When all are gone,
Like inhabitants;

These migrant birds
With white stars
Painted
On their foreheads
Land always among the homeless.

II.

Dark shape
Under a white hat,
I can only dream you,
Dream you and believe
The shape my mind conjures,
The breeze my body knows,
For you are what it is to see
And what it is to reach through night
And know
The cold has been warned.

III.

As white flags are lowered
Over green forts,
What sinks in me
Who calls himself *I*
But knows better,
Embraces you,
Who are not there either.

A CHRYSALIS

On your silky
Young
Woman's belly
Throbs
With a mind of its own

In which I wish
I lay like a pulse
Keeping time with your heart.

Instead
I catch
My quick
Chitinous
Breath.

(Mellowing
In your hair, I
The pathetic pupa
Burst:

Under
       The
              Branch
Of
A
Tree
Lies
The spent
Cocoon).

The
W
O
R
M
Is
A
Butterfly.

COMPASS

How hard
The bud of your sex

In love
When your eye's sharpened stare
Fixes
Like a dagger

The four quarters
Of my heart,

For this is your answer
To the swollen vein:

A vicious war,
Despite me,
Despite you.

FEMME FATALE

The lake is frozen rock-solid
In the four corners of your heart.
The fish go deep into the channels,
Scrape their bellies on the bottom,
Dare not move.

And if the sun should shine,
Your body would seize-up.
Even now, you hiss, cold-blooded,
Trusting nothing warm.

Still, you play with me
The old game of rock, paper, scissors,
And every time my wrist is slapped
Till the hard corners of your distance
Pierce the open target
Of my heart.

We could go on like this—
Fire and ice forever,
Until one of us is killed.

Instead,
I sharpen my sex like a knife;
You sharpen yours like a pair of scissors:
Our quick edges grate till sparks fly
And we are consumed in the mutual pleasure
Of our pain.

A CHOICE OF PRIDES

Divinely magnified
By innocent despair,
I seek in whole blood
The child in you, surprised
To find it dead.

The pacifist in me
By not fighting back
Has not been destroyed,

For I know the destruction
Of youth, in peace,
Will nurture the will to kill.

So I yield
Knowing your *hubris*
When you are strong
Will make you over-confident
And ruin you.

TIGER, TIGER

The more I know you
The less I know myself.

It is three in the morning.
You return after a night out
To my side of the bed,
The stripes in your back bleeding
From the enormous hate behind the whip.

I ask but you do not answer,
The silence so thick I can cut it
With a knife. But don't. The question
Echoes wall to wall, floor to ceiling,
In the room of my mind,

And I cringe at the violence
I must feel
To please you
Since I don't.

A SINGULARITY

Curly black hairs flame up
Over the dry cleft of your sex.

You are the hole
Nature has a horror of.

And I, the universe
That fills you in.

KISMET

Your austere beauty does not bend,
And your hardened eyes are still.
You do not walk in terror before me,
And nothing but your confidence fascinates
Me under your will. Consequently, nature
Unfolds in you like a blind seed,
And in awful stillness I watch you
Walk with a panther's need
To destroy with sheer violence,
Though your lips be livid and chill.
When will your hurt mouth quiver,
The agony break and lie still?

Never, it seems, till one of us dies,
For in your sober eyes sorrow coils
With a malice that will not spend.
There is no hope that love can be.
It is too late to will. And I
Will blunder my bold meaning
Into your blood, and plunder,
Taking us both under.

For there is nothing to be learned of love
That will not suffer change, or be killed.
It is in my nature to impregnate you
With my own shape, which is your shape,
The single quality of intense desire,
The separateness of each person,
Primordial, in a separate cave.

NOCTURNE

The lights in the house are snuffed out
The moment anyone knocks:

> Grey smoke
> Rises from the chimney,

A cloud's painless thighs
Let it pass through them,

> And over the horizon
> Darkness hovers,

Its wing-tips dancing
Between dying fires.

QUESTION

You got up and left
Nothing but your form
Pressed in the dying
Leaves of grass.

It's as if some death were needed
To accommodate your slippered weight.
Something dying slowly
Had to be given a push.

But tomorrow
Each blade will forget
The feel of your shadow,
And the field will look the same
From far away.

BIRDS OF MEMORY

Now we who go on
Beat our wings till they bleed.

We look for your eyes
Among the salvoes of guns,

And in the blind air,
As your lids part,

The black light in them breaks
The space between

Our wings
Completely:

We fall in you like an absence,
Your own.

THE SMITH

for Robert Bringhurst

I.

Yet, there is this one, naked,
Who forges home his love, who hammers
Not the anvil but the hot mettle cooling,
Even when cold, cold as old questions
Inlaid like jewels
That once were thorns
In the crown of his voyages, cold
As a chameleon catching fire in the brainstem
And flushing the mind like a covey of quail
Till it eagles, ladling the airless dark
With its wings above the unfinished,
Beyond the complete, again and again
Trying for the whole tornado,
The brain gulping like a furnace
Coal and ozone, fire-water and flame,
The mind leaping and seizing stars,
Comets, nebulae, as whole galaxies
Score the valves of his eyes
Into the fugue of bellows and organ,
The nerve chords thundering
That drive the golden head of Hermes,
Shattering the temples
Where once there were wings.

So, with this treasure, he sears,
Puddles and shingles, blooms
The iron wound of her smooth
With all her depths vermiculate, a web.

And though poker and chimney burn and burn
And she quicken, hate-shattered, awe-stricken,
The child of her babbling like the oracle
About beans when the flower and fruit,
The whole tree of her uproots
Until turned inside-out she screams like a Gorgon
Belching the profanities of her dark.
It is then a fountain sweet as warm sake
Pours out of the desert of her heart.

And while she be never so much
Alone, dream-tasting, convulsive,
And he no different, but in her eyes
Appear above knowing, truly god, it is
Beyond her divination and priestly hexameters,

For her revenge be seated in belief
(Just ask Alexander)
That a foreign king will reign over the bedded land
And the headless cone riot the body politik,
Even beyond the blind Byzantine,
Till she has eaten the last leaf of the laurels
And her final gurgle been translated.

II.

As for that other, the instigator
Is flighty, a dandied vulture
Armed with his love, alluring
With sharp glances *sub rasa*,
Sans vision, a sport ashore
At tide-line observing
(Good fortune and mystery prevailing)
Something elegant dying and washed-up

For him to save.

Thus is the warrior vanquished,
For he always leaves the prize like a mortal,
A suitor unable to string or draw the bow,
Unable to know through her what a god is,

And know ye, know ye, gods
If you are, I am
He who loved her more than any man
Did, has since or ever will.

EVE: AN EPILOGUE

She ate it: apple, pear, date;
Grape, olive or fig: whatever grows
Wild like fire and naturally cold
In Babylon, or so far east of Eden it became
Common as hate, as rare as love,
In the west: whatever was forbidden
By a high voice in the cool of the day.

And it ate her, body and mind,
Enough to know she was alone, and naked,
As rare as the fruit, a newly-discovered
Part of herself, if not the fruit itself.
Yes, she was so unique she knew Adam
Was still a child and loved her and would taste
The darkness in the light
And the light in the darkness
Until he became an intolerable grey—
But only because he loved her.
Already she saw it as a weakness.

So she pushed him to the cliff-edge, knowing
Where the tree grew, knowing Adam's green
The only colour the dead love to kill.
And he ate and ate till there was nothing to eat.
And then he ate that too, knowing
A strong love is indeed blind,
Perhaps because it is strong,
And infinitely corruptible.

III.

Near and
Hard to grasp is
The God,
But where danger is,
Deliverance also grows.

Friedrich Holderlin, *from* "Patmos"

PHOENIX

A feather stirs the ashes, grey and white,
The singed fledgling finds only darkness
Retreating, a cooling absence, a distance,
And the smoking cinder of the heart,
All that remains of the fire.

Eyes scored, though not blinded,
He leaps into his new wings
And finds altitude enough,
The pure air, where his mind,
Kiln-dried, gets a bead
On the rocky heights,
The lobes of his brain pumping
Toward the promising light.

NOON WINDOW

Halifax

The day is undecided
Between 12 noon
And 12:01
Whether the grey snails
Will lie pasted to rocks
Or fall like monks on cathedral floors.

Pine trees creak in their trunks,
And warships wait in the harbour.

The water is calm as summer passes
With the skipping stones of boys.

A light turns red.
Big trucks and buses screech behind
A small boy on a bike.

An elephant shrieks, a hyena laughs,
And dark eyes close in the trees.

Relieved, I have no questions.
Sunday has an afternoon.

FOUR SONGS FOR THEA

I.

If you have felt the earth quake
And shake the house and all in it,
That is how my heart beats
Learning the language of your skin.

If you have seen fire in sunlight
Illuminate the yellow bells of the flowers,
That is the way the look in my eyes
Enters your eyes.

If you have heard the wind rush
And whistle in the limbs of a pine tree,
That is how I let my hands
Trace the shape of a woman.

If you have watched an ocean wave rise,
Bend and break into white foam,
That is the way I move over you
And will always come to you.

If you know how I move through
Earth, fire, air and water to find you,
That is the way I will teach my body to teach you
To shape the words rolling off my tongue.

II.

You gaze at me
With the eyes of a doe,
As at the beginning.

A comfortable softness,
The gentle look in your eyes hesitates,
And you move over me carefully
Like a word looking for another word.

I find my hands going more slowly
Over you, pronouncing my own echo
As if it were a part of myself
I have never heard before.

Our tongues touch like eagles
Locking claws in mid-air
And circle each other
Telling all the words we know
Till just above ground we fly
Separately away into the air's arms.

Tonight, to sleep is to remember
My own name which lies
Beside your own name.

III.

You are here; I am here
In the cozy bed at last.

I let my hands journey over all of you,
Comb my fingers through your hair:
I dance with mouth and tongue
All around you as wind around the air.

You let your hair fall all over me,
Hold me in your fingers and thighs.

And I take hold of you finally
Lifting you by your shoulders and knees
And draw your belly down under my own.

You are here; I am here,
And each of us finds within the other
The heart of time in the dying flesh we embrace,
And each of us sheds light on the other
Once upon a time, and for all time.

IV.

Tenderness is loving
Each other's weakness,

And there is no mystery
In how we love or why.

Ours is the gravity
Of the sun

For this blue planet:
Only the heart

Of a star
Beats this big.

SONG FOR MY DAUGHTER

Out of the night of your mother's throat,
Out of her defiled mouth,
Buried under centuries of biblical dark,
And unseen under the lens of truth,
Out come her screams, in words I don't understand
But sense, sounds like hammers beating
The xylophone of my backbones,
And like a desperate ghost,
I hold her hands in my hands,
Giving her something to push against.

As the sun rises at daybreak,
As mist rises in skeins over the Fraser,
As a tree reaches into air for the light,
As the close air is fanned in the room,
As the doctor flashes his scalpel
Under the lamp and cuts as if through bread,

A cry comes out of the atom,
A cry grows vast in the web of starlight,
A cry laughs in a shattering wave,
A cry locks weeping in a pool,
A cry grimaces in bone,
A cry hammers walls and veins,
A cry tries to squeeze out through words,

And you are born.

LIGHT

Out of this I will kill sleep
And build a tower
Too beautiful to tell

And far too beautiful to see,
Whose distance
Is the worst of me.

And this light
Will shine on all my desires;
It will protect my flesh
And fan my constant fire,

For it will crucify with nails
And keep the world bright
And closed the body's sails.

And from this fair edifice
My blazing eyes shall see
The moral grandeur of man
Animating all his days.

And peace will be prize
And purity be grace
To make the human absolute
As sweet as the human face.

It will bring the solemn inward pain
Of truth into the heart again

ABOUT THE AUTHOR

R. W. STEDINGH was born in Camden, New Jersey in 1944. He was educated at Glassboro State College (now Rowan University) and Rutger's University, and from 1966 to 1968, he worked as an English teacher in Swiss private schools. Since then he has become a Canadian citizen and received an M. A. in Creative Writing from the University of British Columbia and started post-graduate work in Comparative Literature at the University of Toronto. From 1970 to 1971 he was Managing Editor of *PRISM international* and from 1970 to 1974, the Founding Editor of the *Canadian Fiction Magazine*. His poetry, fiction and translations from the French, Spanish and Estonian have appeared widely in the English-speaking world. He is the author of three books of poetry, *Faces of Eve, From a Bell Tower* and the third, *The Stanley Park Suite,* is due to appear later this year. He is also the translator (with T. E. Moks) of *Arved Viirlaid: Selected Poems*, which is scheduled for publication next year. He lives in Vancouver.